How Many on the Log?

by
Sydnie Meltzer Kleinhenz

•

illustrated by
Diane Blasius

MODERN CURRICULUM PRESS
Pearson Learning Group

How many on the log?

One frog on the log.

How many on the log?

Two frogs on the log.

How many on the log?

Three frogs on the log.

How many on the log?

Four frogs on the log.

How many on the log?

Five frogs on the log.

How many on the log?

Six frogs on the log.

How many on the log?
One cat on the log!